SOUPS

*Tasty homemade
soups and broths*

*With illustrations of
bygone rural life
by Alfred Quinton*

SALMON

Index

Cover pictures: *front:* Little Comberton, Worcestershire
Back: Ripple, Worcestershire
Title page: Welford-upon-Avon, Gloucestershire

Copyright, Printed and Published by Dorrigo, Manchester, England © Copyright.

Cheese and Onion Soup

This thick, smooth, cheesy soup is complemented by tangy mustard toasts.

1 oz butter	**1 pint milk**
3 medium onions, peeled and finely diced	**½ pint chicken stock or ¼ pint stock**
1 clove garlic, peeled and finely chopped	**and ¼ pint white wine**
1 oz flour	**Salt and pepper**
½ teaspoon dry mustard powder	**4 oz Cheddar cheese, grated**

MUSTARD TOASTS
Thinly sliced bread, toasted on one side only   Butter   Whole Grain Mustard

Melt the butter in a large saucepan, add the diced onions and garlic and cook gently for 10-15 minutes until the onions are soft and transparent but not browned. Add the flour and mustard and cook for 2-3 minutes more. Remove from the heat and gradually add the milk and stock (or stock and wine), stirring all the time. Return to the heat and, stirring continuously, bring to the boil. When the soup thickens reduce the heat and simmer for 5 minutes. Remove from the heat and stir in the cheese. Serve immediately with Mustard Toasts. To make the Mustard Toasts, butter the un-toasted side of the bread and spread generously with mustard. Place under a medium grill for a few minutes until crisp and golden. Cut into fingers and serve with the soup. Serves 4 to 6.

The Village Cross, Ashton under Hill, Gloucestershire

Ham and Pea Soup

A good way of using up a left-over end of a bacon joint.

1 oz butter
1 medium onion, peeled and diced
8 oz potatoes, peeled and diced
12 oz peas, podded

1½ pints chicken or pork stock
8 oz gammon, grilled and cut
   into very small pieces
Pepper

Pinch dried sage and thyme

Melt the butter in a large saucepan, add the onion and potatoes, cover and cook gently for 10 minutes, stirring occasionally. Add the peas and stock, cover and simmer for 10 to 15 minutes until all the vegetables are tender. Cool, purée in a processor or blender and return to the pan. Add the gammon, season with pepper and herbs. Heat thoroughly and serve hot with crusty bread. Serves 4 to 6.

Frozen peas can be used if fresh peas are out of season. If left-over boiled bacon is used then there is no need for it to be grilled.

Watercress Soup

The slightly peppery taste of watercress gives this soup a hint of 'bite'
served chilled on a hot summer day.

1 oz butter	¾ pint chicken stock
1 onion, peeled and finely chopped	½ lb potatoes, peeled and cubed
1 tablespoon flour	1 pint milk
2 bunches watercress, washed	Salt and black pepper
and trimmed	4 to 6 tablespoons double cream

Melt the butter in a saucepan and add the onion. Cook, covered, until soft, but not browned, then stir in the flour. Chop the watercress roughly, reserving a few leaves for garnish and stir into the onion mixture. Cook for 1 to 2 minutes, stirring, then add the stock and the potatoes. Bring to the boil, then cover and simmer for 30 minutes. Allow to cool slightly, then purée in a processor or blender. Return to a clean saucepan and add the milk. Season to taste and re-heat thoroughly. Pour into bowls and serve with a tablespoon of cream swirled into the soup in each bowl and garnish with the reserved watercress leaves. In summer, this soup is delicious served chilled. After re-heating, chill thoroughly before serving garnished as above. Serves 4 to 6.

Crab Soup

A less expensive alternative to 'lobster bisque'.

1 oz butter
2 sticks celery, prepared
   and chopped
1 medium onion, peeled and diced
1 clove garlic, peeled and crushed
¼ pint dry white wine
1 pint good fish stock
1 bay leaf

1 teaspoon anchovy essence
Salt and freshly ground black pepper
1 lb brown and white crab meat
   mixed i.e. the cooked 'meat'
   from two medium size crabs
¼ pint single cream
1 tablespoon brandy
   or 2 tablespoons sherry

Melt the butter in a large saucepan and gently cook the onion, garlic and celery until the onion is soft and transparent but not browned. Add the wine and stock and the bay leaf, anchovy essence, salt and pepper. Boil rapidly for 5 minutes. Add the crab meat and simmer, covered, for a further 10 minutes. Remove the bay leaf and purée in a processor or blender. Return to the pan and add the cream and the brandy or sherry. Warm through, but do not boil and serve. Serves 4.

Turkey Broth

When the roast turkey has been eaten, it is useful to have a means of using the cold remains. This sustaining broth is ideal to come home to after a brisk post-Christmas walk.

2 oz butter	1½ pints chicken stock
1 onion, peeled and finely chopped	Pinch of mixed herbs
1 large carrot, prepared and finely cubed	8 oz cooked turkey, diced
8 oz potato, peeled and cubed	4 oz frozen peas
1 stick celery, prepared and chopped	4 oz frozen runner beans, sliced
1 teaspoon curry powder	½ pint creamy milk
1 oz flour	Parsley
	Salt and pepper
	Pinch of paprika to garnish

Melt the butter in a pan and add all the vegetables except the peas and beans. Stir in the curry powder and cook for a few minutes. Add the flour and gradually stir in the stock. Add the herbs, bring to the boil, cover and simmer gently for 40 minutes. Add the peas, beans and turkey meat and simmer for 15 minutes, then add the milk and parsley and season to taste. When hot, serve in bowls, sprinkling paprika on top of each bowl. Serves 6.

Hampton Ferry, near Evesham, Worcestershire

Cullen Skink

This hearty fishermen's soup from Scotland is, traditionally, always made with smoked Finnan haddock.

1 large Finnan haddock fillet	1 pint full cream milk or buttermilk
1 onion, peeled and chopped	1 oz butter
½ lb mashed potato	Salt and pepper

Place the haddock in a large saucepan with sufficient water to cover. Bring to the boil, add the chopped onion and simmer for 10-15 minutes until the fish is cooked. Remove the fish, retaining the stock and flake the flesh from the bones and skin. Set the flesh to one side and return the bones and skin to the stock. Boil for 30 minutes. Remove from the heat and strain the stock into a clean pan. Add the flaked fish and return to the heat. Add the milk and salt to taste and bring to the boil for a few minutes. Stir in the mashed potato with the butter and pepper to taste and serve immediately. Serves 4.

Onion Soup

This is a clear soup with a more than usual amount of chopped onion.

4 large onions, peeled and finely chopped	**1¾ pints vegetable stock**
	1 teaspoon yeast extract
1 tablespoon oil for frying	**Black pepper**

Heat the oil in a large saucepan and fry the finely chopped onions gently until just softened but not browned. Add the stock and the yeast extract and stir well. Season with plenty of freshly ground black pepper. Bring to the boil, stirring, then cover and simmer gently until the onions are really soft. Serve very hot. Serves 6.

The Walks, Groombridge, Kent

Farmhouse Vegetable Soup

Basic, everyday vegetables make up this chunky, everyday standby soup.

1 lb carrots, prepared and coarsely chopped	**1 leek, prepared and sliced**
	2 oz butter
1 lb onions, peeled and coarsely chopped	**2 lb potatoes, peeled and coarsely chopped**
2 sticks of celery, prepared and chopped	**1 pint lamb stock**
	Bouquet garni

Salt and pepper

Melt the butter in a large saucepan, add the chopped vegetables, except the potatoes and cook for 10 minutes, covered, stirring occasionally, until the vegetables are soft. Put the potatoes, stock, *bouquet garni* and salt and pepper into the pan and add enough water to cover the vegetables. Bring to the boil and simmer for 45 minutes. Remove the *bouquet garni* and serve. The potatoes thicken the soup and may disappear into the liquid. The vegetables may be diced or finely chopped using a food processor, as preferred. Serves 4.

Laver Soup

Laver, a red-coloured edible seaweed collected from the rocks around the Welsh coast, is used to make this nourishing, thick vegetable soup.

4 oz butter	**3 oz laverbread**
2 medium onions, peeled and chopped	**2 pints lamb stock**
3 medium potatoes, peeled and chopped	**Salt and black pepper**
1 medium carrot, prepared and chopped	**½ level teaspoon caster sugar**

A little chopped fresh parsley for garnish

Melt the butter in a large saucepan and cook the vegetables, covered, until lightly browned. Stir in the laver and the stock, bring to the boil and simmer, covered, for 20 to 30 minutes until the vegetables are tender. Allow to cool a little then purée in a processor or blender. Return to a clean saucepan, add the seasoning and sugar and reheat thoroughly. Pour into bowls and serve, garnished with parsley. Serves 4 to 6.

Prepared laver, usually tinned, can be obtained from health food shops, specialist grocers or some supermarkets. If bought fresh it must be washed VERY well in cold, running water to remove all sand and then boiled in water for 30 to 40 minutes and drained thoroughly; at this stage it will look a little like cooked spinach. When cooked it is minced or chopped and it then becomes laverbread, ready for use.

Summer Pea Soup

Freshly podded peas give this delightful soup a fresh taste of summer.
Ideal chilled on that hot, sunny day.

2 oz butter	1 pint vegetable or chicken stock
1 lb shelled peas	4-6 mint leaves
4 oz spring onions, chopped	Salt and freshly ground black pepper
½ lettuce, washed and sliced	1 level teaspoon sugar

Melt the butter in a large saucepan and add the peas, spring onions and lettuce. Cover and cook gently for 10 minutes, being careful not to brown the vegetables. Add the stock, mint and sugar, season with salt and pepper and cook until the peas are tender. Purée in a processor or blender until quite smooth. This soup is delicious served either hot or chilled, perhaps with a little cream and a scattering of snipped chives. Serves 4.

Mulligatawny Soup

This is a curry-flavoured soup of Anglo-Indian origin.

1½ lbs stewing lamb	2 carrots, prepared and sliced
3 pints water	2 onions, peeled and sliced
1½ oz dripping or lard	½ lb tomatoes
½ teaspoon salt	3 dessertspoons flour
¼ teaspoon cayenne pepper	3 dessertspoons curry powder

A glass of Madeira wine

Melt the dripping or lard in a large saucepan and cook the carrots and onions until lightly browned. Stir in the flour and curry powder and cook for a few more minutes. Cut the lamb into small pieces, cut up the tomatoes and add both to the vegetables. Add the water with seasoning to taste. Bring slowly to the boil. Remove the scum and simmer, covered, for about two and a half hours. Take out the meat and purée the soup in a processor or blender. Allow to get quite cold and then remove the fat from the top of the soup. Reheat the soup and adjust the seasoning. Before serving add the Madeira wine. Serves 6 to 8.

Carhampton, Somerset

Cockle Soup

Soups made with this ubiquitous shellfish have always been popular around Britain's coasts.

40 to 50 cockles
1 oz butter
1 small onion, peeled and
   finely chopped
2 heaped tablespoons flour
¾ to 1 pint milk

2 sticks celery, finely chopped
2 tablespoons fresh chopped parsley
Salt and pepper
¼ pint single cream
1 stick celery, trimmed and
   finely chopped for garnish

Wash and scrub the cockles well, discarding any that are open. Place in a large pan with just enough lightly salted water to cover and bring to the boil, shaking the pan from time to time. Cook until the cockles have opened, then remove pan from the heat. When cool enough to handle, strain the cockles, reserving the liquid and remove them from their shells. Melt the butter in a pan and sweat the onion gently until soft, then stir in the flour and cook for 1 minute. Mix together the reserved liquid and milk and gradually add to the flour mixture, stirring until smoothly blended. Add the celery, cook for 5 minutes, then stir in the chopped parsley and season. Bring to the boil, simmer for 2 to 3 minutes then add the cockles and heat through thoroughly. Stir in the cream and heat gently, but do not boil. Garnish with chopped celery. Serves 4 to 6.

Leek Soup

A delicious white soup which can be served either hot or cold.

2 pints chicken stock	1 lb potatoes, peeled and diced
1 lb leeks, prepared and sliced thinly	Salt and pepper
2 oz butter	Pinch of nutmeg
2 oz flour	Pinch of thyme
2 onions, peeled and sliced thinly	3 tablespoons single cream
	Croutons to garnish

Melt the butter in a large saucepan, add the vegetables and cook for a few minutes, stirring, until soft but without browning. Add the flour and gradually stir in the stock. Add the nutmeg, thyme and seasoning. Simmer gently, covered, for about 40 minutes, then purée in a processor or blender. Place in a clean pan and heat through. Just before serving stir in the cream and garnish with croutons. This soup may be served hot or chilled. Serves 6.

Shere, near Guildford, Surrey

Spinach Soup

A beautifully green-coloured soup garnished with red paprika.

1 oz butter	**1 lb fresh spinach leaves**
1 onion, peeled and diced	**1 tablespoon lemon juice**
1 oz flour	**Salt and pepper**
1 ½ pints chicken stock	**2 tablespoons single cream**
1 teaspoon paprika	

Melt the butter in a large saucepan, add the onion and cook gently until soft. Stir in the flour and cook for 3-4 minutes. Remove from the heat and add the chicken stock. Add the spinach leaves and cook for 5 minutes. Purée in a processor or blender, return to the pan and flavour with lemon juice and salt and pepper. Re-heat and serve hot with a swirl of cream in each bowl and a sprinkling of paprika. Serves 4 to 6.

Cocky Leeky Soup

A chicken and leek soup that is a traditional Scottish speciality.

1 small chicken and giblets (2½-3 lb)	2 oz long grain rice
1 onion, peeled and chopped	1 small carrot, prepared and grated
6 leeks, prepared and cut into one inch long pieces	1 teaspoon salt
	3 pints water
	Salt and pepper

1 tablespoon chopped parsley

Place the chicken, giblets and onion in a large saucepan. Add the water and bring to the boil. Cover and simmer for 1½ hours until the chicken is tender. Remove from the heat and skim off any white scum. Take out the giblets and discard. Take out the chicken and strip the meat from the bones. Discard the bones. Return the meat to the stock. Add the leeks, rice and grated carrot. Bring back to the boil, cover and simmer for a further 30 minutes. Season with salt and pepper to taste. Add the parsley before serving. Serves 6 to 8.

Stilton Soup

The King of English cheeses together with cream and wine, gives this luxury soup a rich texture and flavour all its own.

2 oz butter
1 large onion, peeled and
  finely chopped
2 sticks celery, finely chopped
1 carrot, chopped (if desired)
1 clove of garlic, peeled and
  crushed with a little salt
1 oz flour
2 tablespoons white wine

1 to 1½ pints chicken stock
¼ pint milk
4 to 5 oz Stilton cheese, rind
  removed and crumbled
Salt and black pepper
Pinch of grated nutmeg
5 tablespoons single cream
2 tablespoons fresh chopped
  chives or parsley

Melt the butter in a large saucepan and lightly fry the onions, celery and carrot (if desired) until softened but not browned. Add the garlic, then stir in the flour and cook, stirring, for 1 minute. Stir in the wine and the stock, bring to the boil and simmer for 30 minutes. Add the milk, Stilton cheese and seasoning and heat through, stirring, for 1 minute. Purée in a processor or blender and pour into a clean saucepan. Stir in the cream and 1½ tablespoons of the herbs. Heat through, but do not allow to boil. Serve garnished with the remaining herbs. Serves 4 to 6.

Barley Cream Soup

A really simple country recipe which dates from the 18th century.

4 oz pearl barley   **¼ pint double cream**
1¾ pints chicken stock   **Salt and pepper**
¼ pint milk   **1 oz butter**
2 teaspoons chopped parsley

Blanch the barley by placing in a bowl and pouring boiling water on to it. Leave for 1 minute and then drain. Add the drained barley to the chicken stock in a large saucepan and simmer for 2 hours. Purée the barley mixture in a processor or blender and then add to it the milk, cream and the butter cut up into small pieces. Season with salt and pepper. Return to the saucepan, reheat and then serve sprinkled with chopped parsley. Serves 6.

Cottages and church, Monks Eleigh, Suffolk

Asparagus Soup

This delicate, creamy soup is best made with English asparagus, the finest in the world.

A good ½ lb asparagus spears,
   wiped and trimmed
1 pint chicken stock (see note)
3 sprigs parsley and a small bayleaf
   tied together with string
Salt and white pepper

1 teaspoon sugar
1½ oz butter
1½ oz flour
1 pint milk
3 fl.oz double cream
2 teaspoons lemon juice

Chop the asparagus into short lengths, reserving a few tips for garnish. Bring the stock to the boil in a saucepan then add the asparagus pieces, herbs, seasoning and sugar. If desired, a few peas or a little chopped spinach can also be added to the stock to enhance the soup's delicate colouring. Bring back to the boil and simmer, covered, for 30 to 40 minutes. Discard the herbs, allow to cool a little, then sieve or purée in a processor or blender. Melt the butter in a clean saucepan and stir in the flour. Add the milk slowly, stirring all the time until the mixture is smooth, then add the asparagus purée, bring to the boil and simmer, stirring, for 2 minutes. Adjust the seasoning, then stir in the cream and heat through, but do not allow to boil. Serve garnished with the reserved asparagus tips. These tips need to be cooked separately for about 10 minutes in a little boiling water to which 2 teaspoons of lemon juice has been added, then drained well. Serves 4 to 6.

Pheasant Soup

A clear, game soup; just the thing for a dinner party. Not as expensive as it sounds.

1 pheasant, cleaned and jointed
1 large onion, peeled and
   roughly chopped
2 carrots, prepared and sliced
1 leek, prepared and sliced
2 sticks celery, prepared and chopped
6 sprigs parsley, 2 sprigs thyme and
   a bayleaf, tied together with string

1 blade of mace
12 peppercorns
Salt
2 teaspoons lemon juice
4 tablespoons port or sherry
1 stick celery, wiped, trimmed
   and finely diced
1 teaspoon lemon juice

Place the pheasant joints, onion, carrots, leek, celery, herbs, mace and peppercorns in a large saucepan. Add salt to taste and one teaspoonful of the lemon juice. Add sufficient cold water to cover. Bring to the boil, then cover and simmer over a very gentle heat for 4 hours. Strain well, reserving the best pieces of pheasant meat. Allow to get cold, then skim off all the surface fat. Dice the reserved meat. Pour the soup into a saucepan, add the diced pheasant meat and bring to the boil. Stir in the port or sherry. Serve the soup garnished with the finely diced celery, which has been blanched in boiling water to which 1 teaspoon of lemon juice has been added. Serve with fingers of hot toast. Serves 4.

The Village Cross, East Hagbourne, Berkshire

Leek and Oatmeal Broth

This is a very old and filling soup recipe; just the thing for a cold winter day.

1 pint milk	Salt and pepper
1 pint chicken or vegetable stock	4 leeks, trimmed, washed well and
A walnut of butter	cut into 1 inch rings
3 rounded tablespoons oatmeal	2 tablespoons fresh chopped parsley

A little single cream for garnish (optional)

Mix the milk and stock together and pour into a large saucepan. Add the butter, bring to the boil and then add the oatmeal, stirring well. Return to the boil, then simmer for 10 minutes, stirring from time to time. Add the leeks and seasoning, return to the boil, then simmer for a further 15 to 20 minutes, covered, stirring in the parsley a few minutes before the end of the cooking time. Serve in bowls each garnished with a swirl of cream, if desired. Serves 4 to 6.

If preferred, this soup can be puréed in a processor or blender before serving, but it is more usual to serve it 'chunky'.

Winter Vegetable Soup

This warming farmhouse soup can be made from a variety of vegetables,
but leeks and potatoes always predominate.

3 large potatoes, peeled and diced
3 large leeks, prepared and trimmed
1 onion, peeled and chopped
2 carrots, prepared and diced
2 sticks celery, prepared and chopped
½ small turnip, peeled and diced

½ small swede, peeled and diced
1 to 1½ oz butter
1 oz flour
2½ to 3 pints chicken or vegetable stock
Salt and black pepper
A bouquet garni

Fresh chopped parsley for garnish

Melt the butter in a large saucepan, add the vegetables, cover and sweat over a low heat for 5 to 10 minutes. Stir in the flour, then pour in the stock, stirring all the time. Add the seasoning and herbs. Bring to the boil then simmer, covered, for 40 to 50 minutes. Remove the herbs and serve, garnished with parsley and accompanied by crusty bread. If preferred, this soup can be puréed in a processor or blender, enriched with milk or single cream and served garnished with a swirl of cream and chopped parsley. Serves 6 to 8.

Fish Soup

Any mixed, flaky white fish can go into this smooth, creamy white soup.

2 lb mixed white fish	A 'walnut' of butter
1 onion, peeled and chopped	2 tablespoons flour
1 leek prepared and sliced	¼ pint milk
1 stick celery, prepared and chopped	A little grated lemon rind
2 tablespoons tomato purée	1 teaspoon fennel leaves, chopped
4 fluid oz white wine	2 tablespoons parsley, chopped
	Salt and black pepper

Put the fish, onion, leek and celery in a large saucepan and cover with 2 pints of water. Bring to the boil and simmer until the fish is cooked. Lift out the fish and flake coarsely, removing any skin and bones. Return the skin and bones to the saucepan with the vegetables and continue to cook for a further 20 minutes, adding more water if necessary. Strain, and pour the liquid into a clean saucepan. Stir in the tomato purée and the white wine. Melt the butter in a small saucepan and stir in the flour, then gradually add the milk, stirring until smooth. Add the sauce to the fish liquid and cook for 3 to 4 minutes, stirring all the time. Then add the flaked fish, lemon rind and chopped herbs and season to taste. Bring to the boil, stirring lightly and serve at once, garnished with a little extra chopped herbs, if desired. Serves 4 to 6.

Field Mushroom Soup

Although cultivated mushrooms are always available and can be used,
they cannot compete for depth of flavour with mushrooms freshly gathered
in dew-soaked fields in autumn.

1 lb fresh field mushrooms,
washed and sliced roughly
2 medium onions, peeled and
roughly chopped

1 pint chicken or vegetable stock
2 oz butter
2 oz flour
1½ pints full cream milk

Salt and pepper

In a large saucepan, cook the mushrooms and onions in the stock for about 30 minutes until tender, then purée in a processor or blender. Melt the butter in a separate pan, add the flour and cook gently for 2-3 minutes Remove the pan from the heat and gradually stir in all the milk. Bring to the boil and stir until it thickens. Add the purée of mushrooms and return to the heat. Simmer for 30 minutes, season well and serve. Serves 6.

Martyrs' Worthy, near Winchester, Hampshire

Cheshire Soup

*A cheese flavoured potato soup which can also be served as
a quick and satisfying meal.*

1 pint pork stock
10 oz potatoes, peeled and
   diced - weighed after peeling
2 leeks, washed, trimmed and
   finely chopped

2 carrots, prepared and grated
Salt and black pepper
1 oz pinhead oatmeal
2 oz grated cheese,
   preferably Cheshire

Put the stock into a large saucepan, add the potatoes, leeks, carrots and seasoning and bring to the boil. Simmer for 15 minutes, or until the vegetables are soft. Sprinkle in the oatmeal and simmer for a further 10 minutes or until the soup has thickened. Just before serving, stir in half the grated cheese. Pour into soup bowls, sprinkle on the remaining cheese and serve. Serves 4.

Pea Soup

Dried peas, carrots, leeks and onions are readily available for this rich, creamy 'stand-by'.

1 lb dried peas	1 rasher bacon, finely chopped
1 bay leaf	1 leek, prepared and chopped
1 sprig of thyme	1 pint milk
1 sprig of mint	Salt and pepper
1 carrot, prepared and sliced	Chopped mint to garnish
1 onion, peeled and chopped	Double cream
Croûtons	

Soak the dried peas overnight in cold water. Next day, put the soaked peas into a large saucepan and add 2 pints of water. Add all the remaining ingredients except the milk and seasoning. Bring to the boil, cover and simmer for 2 hours. Purée in a processor or blender and return to the pan. Heat the milk nearly to boiling point, add to the purée and season to taste with salt and pepper. Reheat and sprinkle with a little chopped mint. Add a dessertspoon of double cream to each bowl as it is served and garnish with croûtons. Serves 4.

Mill Street, Warwick

Parsnip Soup

A full-flavoured soup based on the humble parsnip.

1 lb parsnips, prepared and diced	1 tablespoon cooking oil
1 onion, peeled and roughly chopped	1 oz flour
2 sticks celery, prepared and diced	2 pints chicken stock
2 oz butter	Salt and pepper

Juice of ½ lemon (according to taste)

Heat the butter and oil in a large saucepan and cook the vegetables, covered, over a low heat for about 10 to 15 minutes, stirring occasionally, until soft but not browned. Stir in the flour and continue cooking, stirring, for a few more minutes. Add the stock, season with salt and pepper and bring to the boil, stirring. Cover and simmer for about 5 minutes then purée in a processor or blender. Return to the pan, add lemon juice according to taste, check the seasoning and reheat. Serve with a swirl of cream in each bowl. Serves 4 to 6.

The lemon juice is added to counter the sweetness of the parsnips and the amount to be included is simply a matter of personal preference.

Scotch Broth

Originally mutton was always used for this traditional Scottish broth, but today lamb is most likely to be available. Mutton, of course, gave the broth a stronger flavour.

1 lb neck of mutton or lamb	1 onion, peeled and chopped
2½ pints water	1 small carrot, prepared and grated
1 small turnip, peeled and chopped	1 oz cabbage, shredded
1 leek, prepared and chopped	1 oz pearl barley
1 large carrot, prepared and chopped	Chopped parsley to garnish

Place the meat in a large saucepan with the water. Add the pearl barley. Season with salt and pepper. Bring to the boil, cover and simmer for 1 hour. Skim off any white scum. Add the chopped vegetables, cover and simmer for another 1 hour, adding the grated carrot and the cabbage for the final 30 minutes of cooking. Before serving, remove the meat and bones and discard the bones. The meat can be returned to the broth or eaten separately, if preferred. Bring back to the boil and serve, garnished with chopped parsley. Serves 4 to 6.

Carrot Soup

A rich, thick and satisfying vegetable soup.

1 lb carrots, prepared and chopped	1½ pints chicken stock
2 sticks celery, prepared and chopped	A bouquet garni
1 small onion, peeled and finely chopped	Pinch of freshly grated nutmeg
4 oz turnips, peeled and diced	2 oz flour
1 rasher bacon, chopped	¼ pint milk
1 oz butter	2 tablespoons single cream
	Chopped parsley for garnish

Melt the butter in a pan and fry the bacon and vegetables for a few minutes. Transfer to a saucepan, add the stock and the *bouquet garni* (tied to the pan handle for easy removal later) and season well. Cover and simmer gently for about 45 minutes. Remove the *bouquet garni* and then purée the mixture in a processor or blender. Place in a clean pan and re-heat. Add the nutmeg. Blend the flour and milk to a smooth cream and gradually add to the pan, stirring over a low heat until it thickens. Check the seasoning. Just before serving, stir in the cream and sprinkle with a garnish of chopped parsley. Serves 4 to 6.

Broad Bean Soup

Use young, tender, freshly-shelled beans, if possible, for this delicious, creamy textured soup.

2 oz butter	**1 tablespoon caster sugar**
2 medium onions, peeled	**2 pints chicken stock**
and diced	**¼ pint dry white wine or dry sherry**
2 lb shelled broad beans	**3-4 sage leaves**
	Salt and pepper

Melt the butter in a large saucepan and add the onions, broad beans and sugar, Cover and cook gently for 10 minutes, stirring occasionally until the onions are soft but not browned. Add the stock, sage leaves and wine or sherry. Simmer for 30-40 minutes, covered, until the beans are tender. Cool slightly and purée in a processor or blender. If a very smooth texture is required the soup may be sieved after liquidizing. Return the soup to the pan, taste and season with salt and freshly ground black pepper. Serves 6.

Cottage at Tillington, near Petworth, Sussex

Potato Soup

This farmhouse soup contains two traditional ingredients, potatoes and bacon.

2 rashers streaky bacon, derinded and chopped
1 oz butter
1½ lb potatoes, peeled, chopped and weighed after peeling
2 onions, peeled and chopped
1½ pints chicken stock

½ pint milk
6 sprigs parsley, tied together
Salt and white pepper
¼ pint single cream
1 rasher streaky bacon, de-rinded, chopped and fried until crisp
Fresh chopped parsley for garnish

Gently fry the bacon in a large saucepan until the fat begins to run, then add the butter, potatoes and onions and cook, stirring, for 10 minutes. Add the stock, milk, parsley sprigs and seasoning, bring to the boil and then cover and simmer for 30 to 40 minutes, or until the vegetables are tender. Allow to cool slightly, remove the parsley sprigs, then purée in a processor or blender. Return to a clean saucepan, stir in the cream and heat through thoroughly, without boiling. Serve in bowls, garnished with the chopped fried bacon and the chopped parsley. Serves 4 to 6.

Celery Soup

Celery is now available at most times of the year and this recipe is garnished with grated cheese.

1½ oz butter	1 pint chicken stock
1 head celery, wiped, and finely chopped	½ pint milk
1 onion, peeled and finely chopped	Pinch of caster sugar
1 rasher streaky bacon, derinded	Salt and black pepper
and finely chopped	Pinch of grated nutmeg
1 oz flour	5 tablespoons single cream

A little grated cheese - preferably Red Leicester - for garnish

Melt the butter in a large saucepan and lightly cook the celery, onion and bacon until softened but not browned. Stir in the flour and cook, stirring, for 1 minute. Stir in the stock, bring to the boil and simmer for 15 minutes. Add the milk, sugar and seasoning and simmer for a further 15 minutes. Purée in a processor or blender and pour into a clean saucepan. Heat through, stirring in 4 tablespoons of cream, but do not allow to boil. Serve with the remaining cream swirled lightly into each bowl and garnish with grated cheese. Serves 4.

Bonhill, near Lynton, Devon

Summer Soup

A chilled soup made with the freshest of summer vegetables.

1 oz butter
2 onions, peeled and
  finely chopped
1 large potato, peeled and diced
½ medium cucumber, peeled
  and cubed
1 medium lettuce, washed and
  cut into ½ inch strips

4 oz fresh spinach, washed
  and chopped
1 oz fresh peas, weighed after shucking
A bouquet garni with a curl of lemon rind
1¾ to 2 pints chicken or vegetable stock
1 teaspoon lemon juice
Salt and white pepper
½ pint double cream

Fresh peas, cooked and cooled and fresh chopped mint and parsley, for garnish

Melt the butter in a large saucepan and lightly cook the onion until soft, but still transparent. Add the remainder of the vegetables, herbs and lemon rind, then pour over the stock and lemon juice and season. Bring to the boil, then reduce the heat and simmer, covered, for 30 to 40 minutes. Remove the *bouquet garni* and allow the soup to cool completely. Purée in a processor or blender and adjust the seasoning, if necessary. Reserving two tablespoons of cream, stir the remainder into the soup and chill for at least 1 hour before serving. Pour into bowls and garnish each with a swirl of cream, a few peas and a sprinkling of mint and parsley Serves 4 to 6.

Carrot and Leek Soup

A carrot and leek soup thickened with potato and spiced with curry powder.

1oz butter
1 lb leeks, prepared and sliced
1 lb carrots, prepared and sliced

1 medium potato, peeled and chopped
½ level teaspoon curry powder
2 pints chicken stock

Salt and pepper

Melt the butter in a large saucepan and add the vegetables. Cover and cook very gently for 10 minutes without browning. Add the curry powder and cook for 2 minutes, stirring and then add the stock. Bring to the boil, reduce the heat and simmer for 30 minutes, covered, until the vegetables are tender. Cool slightly and purée in a processor or blender. Return to the pan, season to taste and reheat to serve. Serves 4 to 6.

Oxtail Soup with Rice and Barley

A rich meaty soup, almost a meal in itself.

1 lb oxtail	2 pints beef stock
2 oz butter	8 peppercorns
2 onions, chopped	2 cloves
2 sticks of celery, chopped	1 medium carrot, grated
2 oz lean ham or bacon, small cubed	1 tablespoon rice
1 bay leaf	2 tablespoons barley
A bouquet garni	A small glass of sherry

1 tablespoon cornflour

Roll oxtail pieces in seasoned flour and fry in butter, a few pieces at a time, until sealed all over. Add onion and celery to pan with ham or bacon and fry all together until nicely browned. Transfer to large saucepan, add stock and herbs, peppercorns and cloves, bring to boil and simmer very gently, covered, for 4 hours. Strain liquid and leave to get quite cold, preferably overnight. When cold, take off fat. Meanwhile, discard bones, cut up lean meat of oxtail into very small pieces and reserve. Put strained soup into saucepan and add grated carrot, rice and barley and simmer for 1 hour until barley is well cooked. Mix cornflour with sherry, add to soup and bring to boil, stirring until thickened. Add oxtail meat last of all, season to taste and continue cooking to re-heat oxtail. Serve hot. Serves 6.

METRIC CONVERSIONS

The weights, measures and oven temperatures used in the preceding recipes can be easily converted to their metric equivalents. The conversions listed below are only approximate, having been rounded up or down as may be appropriate.

Weights

Avoirdupois	Metric
1 oz.	just under 30 grams
4 oz. (¼ lb.)	app. 115 grams
8 oz. (½ lb.)	app. 230 grams
1 lb.	454 grams

Liquid Measures

Imperial	Metric
1 tablespoon (liquid only)	20 millilitres
1 fl. oz.	app. 30 millilitres
1 gill (¼ pt.)	app. 145 millilitres
½ pt.	app. 285 millilitres
1 pt.	app. 570 millilitres
1 qt.	app. 1.140 litres

Flour as specified in these recipes refers to plain flour unless otherwise described.